SONG OF THE SPARROW

Nature Vignettes Through Lens & Thought

DEBORAH FREEMAN

Balboa Press books may be ordered through booksellers or by contacting:

Balboa Press
A Division of Hay House
1663 Liberty Drive
Bloomington, IN 47403
www.balboapress.com
1 (877) 407-4847

ISBN: 978-1-9822-0802-8 (sc)
ISBN: 978-1-9822-0803-5 (e)

Library of Congress Control Number: 2018908145

Print information available on the last page.

Balboa Press rev. date: 07/27/2018

BALBOA.
PRESS
A DIVISION OF HAY HOUSE

Introducing myself

When I was young I would wake up Friday mornings with the feeling of excitement. This was the day we would leave for the country and I could be outside ... everything was better there. Food tasted better, our family was happier, jokes seemed funnier, life was just more enjoyable. I have spent most of my adult life wanting every day to be Friday.

The stories I have recorded in this book are my way of sharing my Fridays. Nature is a place where every day is Friday for me. I get lost in the joy, the anticipation, the excitement of life. The one thing I have noticed is that there is nearly always purpose in nature. Few things are frivolous. The observations I have made are attempts to share intimate moments of joy, activity, awe and yes, sometimes fear.

When I sit and watch the mother and baby seals playing, the love is palpable. The call of the baby seeking its mother, "Maaaaa" echoing all night long, up and down the shoreline is a haunting call that feeds my soul all year long. The baby might get caught on the rocks by the receding tide, but the mother never leaves the site until they are reunited.

I rejoice in the repeated patterns. Eagles often return to the same nests year after year; the Song Sparrow singing from the same perch right outside our tent follows us down the trail as we make our morning coffee on the rocks by the sea (she loves an audience). Then of course there are the plants ... the beautiful works of art that they are ... the healing they provide, so rich and exquisite in their uniqueness. The joy of greeting them year after year like old friends and the sadness we feel when we know their time is coming to an end and that it will be another year before we see them again. Rhythms, cycles, all good, all necessary.

Then there are the geometric shapes. The designs of feather patterns in birds, seed formations in plants, rock formations on the hillsides, all providing textures and tapestry for our eyes to explore. One thing I have noticed time and again is how often the "heart-shape" is found in all of nature not to mention the repetitions of complex geometric designs.

The photographs in this book were taken with great care and attention. I feel the best of our inner-selves is connected to all of nature; and in sharing these moments I hope to capture the excitement, and present a point of reference for the stories that are told. Some pictures may have been taken several years ago but each picture is particular to the event.

Every day walking in our parks, paddling our waters, listening to the bird-song, enjoying nature wherever we are, can be Friday.

To be a witness is to remember; how the wind feels on our faces, how the sun warms our bodies and how we are a part of a most precious universe. To understand and feel this, is to know how to sing the "Song of the Sparrow".

Contents

In photography light is everything ... but what I have come to realize is that light is everything in all of life ... it's not only a way of seeing it is a way of feeling, of receiving, of maintaining balance.

Illuminations

The art of catching light.
Shimmering, glimmering, sparkling,
bright, dappled, flat, creamy, veiled.
It's all illusive.

Constantly changing.
Constantly presenting challenges.
Mesmerizing, enchanting.
Creating moments of magic.
Creating moments of panic.
Moving quickly from inviting to
inhospitable.

We tend to believe it is weather,
but perhaps it is light, as a
smile turns to a frown.

Our World

(My notebook.)

Lichen 95% fungus – 5% plant.
Lichen eats fairy puke.
Endocrinites defend plants from animals.
Network of fungus connects all plants.

I hear the frog croak in the distance.
I hear the eagle calling its mate to join her for dinner.
I hear the seal splash in the bay.
Joy oh Joy!

We think we are isolated;
but all these sounds, these underground worlds,
these flowing waters, these harsh winds,
this warming sun.

This is our world.
We are deeply connected.

The Event

Part of my heart breaks
When I leave.

I lacked the courage to stay –
to free-fall into the world of words
and light.
I would have loved to continue
to watch you both learning to fly
Your mother, ever the protector,
keeps watch.

The two of you sat for the longest time.

Sometimes side by side,
occasionally facing one another.
I was afraid for you.
We found one dead once, at the foot of its nest-
so far up.

We watched whenever
we could make it to your island-
if the winds were kind.

I wished I was an artist and could draw
your ochre talons and beaks.
Your layers
of deep, tawny, brown, feathers
pushed by the wind.
The same wind
that often kept us away.

I felt like a voyeur.
Neither of you
invited us to watch,
to share,
to be a part of this.
You might think
how typically human to just assume
it would be alright.

I feel somewhat guilty-
but at the same time compelled
to share your event.

Your transition.

5

When I first started taking macro photography seriously I felt like a whole new world had opened-up. I was studying the healing abilities of native plants on Vancouver Island and the lens revealed the magic within both the plants and me.

The Macro

The Macro Lens sees
what I always felt.

I wait all year long to hear this call ... it could be anyone's baby ... maaaa.

Calls in the Night

We listened to your cries
all night long.
It was hard to tell which
one was your mama
and which
was you.

You nestle into her underbelly.
Sometimes she allows.
Sometimes she is annoyed.

We all get annoyed with our children.

But when she turns to you,
she is present and caring.
She raises her head –
a lifting of her body ... a periscope,
making sure it is safe for you to roam.

One thing that is difficult about wildlife photography is trying to do it as unobtrusively as possible. I am at peace in the forest and sometimes fail to realize my presence may cause angst to the very creatures that I so treasure.

Acceptance

I saw you this morning
young mama.
Your baby saw me first,
she was nervous.
You were complacent.

She ran away but you continued
your breakfast.
I was happy to be
accepted
by you.

I was sorry to have made her
anxious.
Maybe tomorrow
she will
accept
me too.

I'm always writing something down. Sometimes revisiting notes I have in books from 30 years ago, then rewritten today. But you have to be in that place of calm … maybe it's the place of enjoying, being a part of the moment.

The Pencil

I'm sitting below
your nest.
I have found
my pencil again.

For a long time it was
buried at the bottom
of my pack
along with my gloom.

I found it today
along with my joy.

Happy to be able
to put it
to use.

This is the "dipper", I call it the little grey bird because if you didn't know it was the one that brought the river to life with its high-pitched call and incredible curious nature, you would think it was JUST a little LGB.

LGB (Little Grey Bird)

Not much of a title
for one so busy.

Head up.
Head down.

Rock to rock.
Leaf to leaf.

Great big maple leaves.
With see-thru veins.

You avoid the sun
so as not to be seen.

I sit and wait
and wait ...
for you to make your way
up the river.

To a sunny patch.

Almost violent in its
brightness.

Smile.

Have you ever........

I think and rethink
of how to tell this story.

To make it real
even to myself.

We had seen the two young elk
from our boats the day before.
Lazily basking in the
warm
morning
sun.

Our boats were silently
gliding upstream.
We got so close
we could see the
tenderness in their
eyes.

But this particular morning,
this same sun
was still quite low in the sky
blocking our view up the river.

All I could see were sparkles,
moving sparkles,
large,
moving sparkles.

The elk?
I turned my boat for a better view.
More shimmering sparkles.

Then it happened.

Have you ever heard a sound ...
a quickening ...
that passed over your insides,
fear, excitement, awe, heart pounding?

It was the howl of the Alpha wolf.

Such a privilege.

Some days it was too turbulent for us to tackle the churning ocean. Then some days we would be so afraid of missing their grand opening, we would go anyway.

Prickly Adventures

It all started with trying to understand
plants, animals, interaction.

Then I met Prickly Pear Cactus.

Such juxtaposition.
Spines so sharp and penetrating.

Rose
so soft
with velvet petals.

Have they opened yet?

These plants can survive any catastrophe
and give us the strength
to do the same.

We were sitting on a rock looking out at the wind-swept trees, discussing how they veer with the prevailing wind ... my thought was isn't that the way we are too??? We move with the wind ... we are all reflections of nature.

Reflections

We are all reflections
of our immediate environment.
Trees, people, all things ...
We move away from the difficult side,
towards the more forgiving.

We can visit these islands year-round if the winds are favorable, but generally we would not attempt to go that far out into the bay until spring. Winter winds are usually too strong for a crossing. They are uninhabited by humans so we feel a responsibility to tread softly and return anything we might have dishevelled to its natural state as much as possible. The flowers, the birds, the rawness of these islands enables us to experience the elements in all their unpredictability and power.

Hebrides

I have always wanted to explore the Hebrides,
ever since I was charmed by Beckwith.

I realize how I have my own version,
my own experience,
on this most special island.

Few trees, harsh winds,
blowing the little hairs on my lover's face.

Once, we both crawled under the tiniest
Arbutus tree,
just for a spot of shade.

Calm at times, all the sparkling eyes of the world
reflected in surrounding miles of ocean.

The turkey vultures circle above in kettles.
You can hear the power of the wings
above the force of the winds.

By The River

My heart beats faster as I approach.
I try not to step on them,
somehow it feels disrespectful,
but there are so many.

The pungent smell of decaying salmon,
eyes missing,
a delicacy in the gull world.

It is the gulls that I hear first.
Their cacophony
creates my excitement.

The bears come.
The fish dangle from their mouths,
like Christmas ornaments,
red and shimmery.

The eagles come
young and old,
the calls, the calls,
the haunting calls.

They line the trees, more than I can count,
more than I can see,
blended into the stage,
hiding behind craggy branches.

What's going on
by the river today?

A banquet
with important guests

Wondering

Today is a remnant of summer
even though it is late September.
We swam or maybe dipped is the better verb,
our skin tingling with the cold saltwater.
We are drying on the rocks and you appear.

A squeal draws my attention to you.
Not the usual drawn out "maaaa" but almost a squeal of rubber tires
stopping too quickly.

You don't shy away. You approach without fear.
Sniffing my kayak, but no,
it's not the one that attracts.

You sniff the other one ... and it is the one you seek.
You sniff and sniff and sniff.

Are you the one we found earlier;
separated from your ma when the tide receded?
The kayak owner had put water on you so you could last
until your mother found you when the tide came back in.

Was it this act of kindness that brought you back?

For years my friend and I would enjoy a cup of tea with sugar cookies as an after school treat ...
then I thought of how the bees would see it. Was this their after school, working hard collecting
pollen treat? These plants dot the islands of the Salish Sea with their bright yellow flowers.

Gummyweed

Covered in frosting before you bloom ...
if you were a cake, a muffin or even a tart,
you would be placed in plastic packaging.

Bees love you.

Do they find you to be sweet and
welcoming, like tea with sugar
accompanied by a Voortman's sugar cookie
at your best friend's house?

Intimate Moments

I'm always searching for you
but today the river was cold looking
and quiet.
No calling, no chatter.

Motion, felt, rather than seen.
Wing span enormous, low to the water,
flying along the river basin.
Lickety-split!

I wondered where you were going.
Then I saw you fold into the river...
body, head. feathers separated, white, grey, black.
Droplets hanging precariously from
your beak.

I felt like a voyeur, climbing down the river bank,
but I had to see this most intimate moment.
This beautiful majestic bird,
Taking a bath.

Then you looked up.

The eyes said:

"Do you mind?"

Everyone likes their privacy.

Kingfisher

I hear your call ... the trill,
a sound
so distinctive that there is
no doubt it is you.

I know if I don't look up quickly
I might miss you.
You're not one to stay long.

My eyes lingered on a Mimulous;
I paid the price.
Catching blue sunlit
tail-feathers in my
peripheral vision.

The Trail

I often walk this trail.

This turn never ceases
to arrest my pace.

The lake, the Arbutus,
the Garry Oak, the golden grasses,
spring flowers, fall sheddings,
translucent light.

I still look for the beaver,
though I think the old timer
said he was dead.

Once I saw an immature eagle
balanced on a sunlit deadhead.
I wanted to sit and watch.
My friends continued their discussion,
heads down, unaware,
so I followed.

I have never seen that sight again.
Now I go alone.

The Dance Of The Setting Sun

They are a work of art ... an arrow.

Tucked wings,
body aligned
perfectly.

The target swimming inches below,
the relentless
wind tossed waves.

They dive, head first,
coming up, head first.
How do they do that?
What do they do
under the water?

Fractions, it all takes
fractions of seconds ...

Climbing out of the water
you see the prize,
and it does ...

The Dance of the Setting Sun.

Regal Morning Guests

Each step deliberate and arched.
Wary eyes, keen observers.

Tufts of white under the chin,
nose outlined with black
nestled in the soft browns
of the coat.

The two bucks are elders,
deserving of respect.

The doe is more calm than they.
She has been before and is in no hurry;
her trust measured by her frequent
nibbles of fallen apples.

The slowly approaching light
of the sun rising,
has presented this fall morning ...
A gift.

Such a way to greet the day.

I can hear them flying across the bay ... so gregarious, always bowing in pleasure when another lands ... they make me wish we as humans could be so open and receiving of one another.

Oyster Catcher's Chatter

You are meant to be
seen and heard.

Your bright red beaks
are instant smile makers.

Like a baby
laughing!

The Eagle

Classic, calm, collected.
Perched, observing, surveying.
So much we can learn from their
Being.

Oh don't be fooled.
They move when there is need.

How many hours have I just watched,
waiting for them to move,
take off, land, feed.

Now I realize the lesson is
in just in being there.

Am I stating the obvious??? I don't think a person can ever be told too often that they are loved.

Love

All love has its value.

The place
inside us
that it fits.

Familiar, warm, accepting

Acknowledgements

My sincere gratitude to my partner Phil Niel, who has accompanied me on many of my adventures and shown me so many interesting aspects of the natural world. He would often point out possible photographic opportunities which, I, in my excitement may have missed. I so value the discussions we have had over the years of how humans, wildlife and plants interact. His excitement at the blooming of the Prickly Pear Cactus and his determination to reach them even in unfavourable winds will be a memory I will always cherish.

To my friends who have given me perspective. Many of whom have dedicated time to various causes to improve our planet, I say thank you and I hope you will see this as my humble contribution. To Morganne Pickering and Diana Mongeau for their years of sharing thoughts and insights.

To Balboa Press for their interest in this project but mostly for how they continue to share lesser known authors with the world in the hopes of offering perspective and ways of seeing this beautiful world that we live in.

To my many Flickr friends (a photography posting site) who have offered much in guiding my own photography experience. Their knowledge and tireless documentation of wildlife in beautiful and unique ways has given me something to strive for in my own work.

To those who have read this book a heartfelt thank you for sharing this journey with me.

Deborah

Bee in Camas flower

A ladybug seeking refuge from the spring rains in a Devil's Club Flower. This plant is a true treasure of nature revered for its healing powers.

Printed in the United States
By Bookmasters